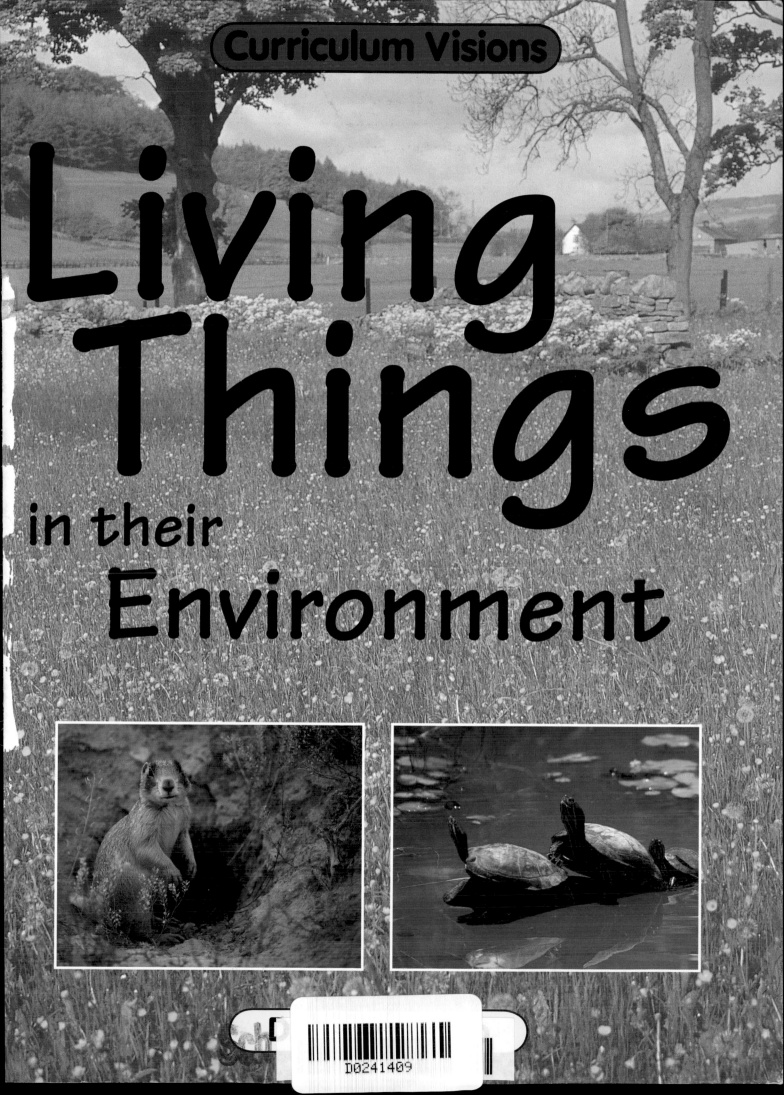

Living Things

in their

Environment

✦ Atlantic Europe Publishing

First published in 2003 by
Atlantic Europe Publishing Company Ltd.

Copyright © 2003
Atlantic Europe Publishing Company Ltd.

Author
Dr Brian Knapp, BSc, PhD

Art Director
Duncan McCrae, BSc

Senior Designer
Adele Humphries, BA, PGCE

Editors
Lisa Magloff, BA, and Gillian Gatehouse

Designed and produced by
EARTHSCAPE EDITIONS

Scans by
EARTHSCAPE EDITIONS and Global Graphics sro

Printed in Hong Kong by
Wing King Tong Company Ltd.

**Living Things in their Environment
– *Curriculum Visions***
**A CIP record for this book is
available from the British Library**

Paperback ISBN 1 86214 309 9
Hardback ISBN 1 86214 311 0

Illustrations
All illustrations by *David Woodroffe*

Picture credits
All photographs are from the Earthscape
Editions photolibrary.

*This product is manufactured from sustainable
managed forests. For every tree cut down at least one
more is planted.*

Lichens living in a harsh mountain habitat

Curriculum Visions

Glossary
There is a glossary on pages 46-47.
Glossary terms are referred to in the
text by using CAPITALS.

Index
There is an index on page 48.

Teacher's Guide
There is a Teacher's Guide to
accompany this book, available
only from this publisher.

Dedicated Web Site
There's more about other great
Curriculum Visions packs and a wealth
of supporting information available at
our dedicated web site. Visit:

www.CurriculumVisions.com

⚠ Be considerate!
If you handle any living thing during your
studies, remember it IS a living thing and should
be treated with consideration and returned to
its environment as soon as possible.

Contents

Plants flowering in the desert

Summary

There are a huge number of different kinds of living thing on the Earth. They all survive here because they are adapted to different environmental conditions. When we change these conditions, we threaten the survival of many life forms. By studying living things in their environment, we can help all living things to survive.

❶ The living things in the **ENVIRONMENT** are called living **ORGANISMS**. They can be divided into three groups – plants, animals and **MICRO-ORGANISMS** (microbes). Although these living things are very different, they share some common features. Find out about them on pages 6 and 7.

❷ Every living thing has a **LIFE CYCLE**. As it goes through its life cycle, a living thing stays **ADAPTED** to its surroundings. Find out how on pages 8 and 9.

❸ Plants have many adaptations to survive. These include producing larger amounts of seeds and having sharp spines and thorns. Find out about them on pages 10 and 11.

❹ Animals have special adaptations to allow them to eat certain kinds of food. Compare these adaptations on pages 12 and 13.

❺ Plants and animals live together in **COMMUNITIES**. Find out what every community needs on pages 14 and 15.

❻ **FOOD CHAINS** show how plants and animals are linked together by the way animals feed. Examine some food chains from a pond community and a land community on pages 16 and 17.

❼ The natural home of a living thing is called its **HABITAT**. Discover how habitats work for many living things on pages 18 to 23.

❽ A pond is a still water habitat that teems with life. Some of the living things are so small that you need a microscope to see them. Take a look on pages 24 and 25.

❾ The speed of river water changes along the river's length. Compare the habitats this creates on pages 26 and 27.

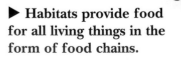

▶ Habitats provide food for all living things in the form of food chains.

▼ Communities exist on all scales, for example on a leaf.

⓭ Meadows and fields are made by farmers for their livestock, but they are also habitats for many different kinds of plants and animals. Discover them on pages 34 and 35.

⓮ People change habitats to suit their own needs. When they do, they can destroy the plants and animals that live there. Find out how on pages 36 and 37.

⓯ Environments can be improved by using our knowledge of how different plants and animals live. See how a country park is designed on pages 38 and 39.

⓰ You can investigate plants in a habitat by simply looking at them. Find out what to look for in different habitats on pages 40 to 45.

⓾ Rock pools are exciting sea water habitats. Find out about the strangely shaped living organisms that survive in them on pages 28 and 29.

⓫ There are harsh weather conditions on mountains, but even so, many plants and animals are adapted to survive there. Discover them on pages 30 and 31.

⓬ Deserts often appear to be lifeless places, but some plants and animals have become adapted for living there. Find out how they survive on pages 32 and 33.

▼ Habitats are complicated, with many types of plants and animals living together.

Weblink: www.CurriculumVisions.com/livingThings

What are living things?

Living things are those things which can produce offspring. Any living thing is called an ORGANISM, but we usually call them by common names, such as plants and animals.

Everything in the world is either living or non-living. An example of a living thing, or organism, is a spider, a cactus or a human being (picture ①). An example of a non-living thing is a piece of rock or a computer. (We use the term non-living instead of dead because, for something to be dead, it must once have been alive. A non-living thing has never been alive.)

Living things can be huge and easy to recognise as being alive, for example, a whale. At the other

▼ ② The difference between the lichen, which is the coloured patch, and the rock, is that the lichen is a living thing, whereas the rock is a non-living thing.

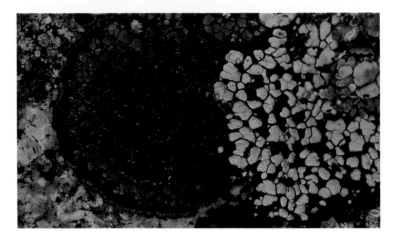

▶ ① How we group living things.

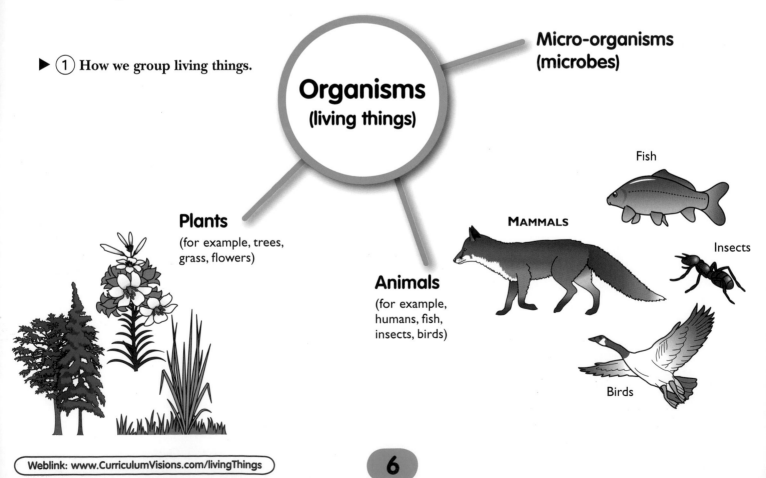

Organisms
(living things)

Micro-organisms
(microbes)

Plants
(for example, trees, grass, flowers)

Animals
(for example, humans, fish, insects, birds)

MAMMALS

Fish

Insects

Birds

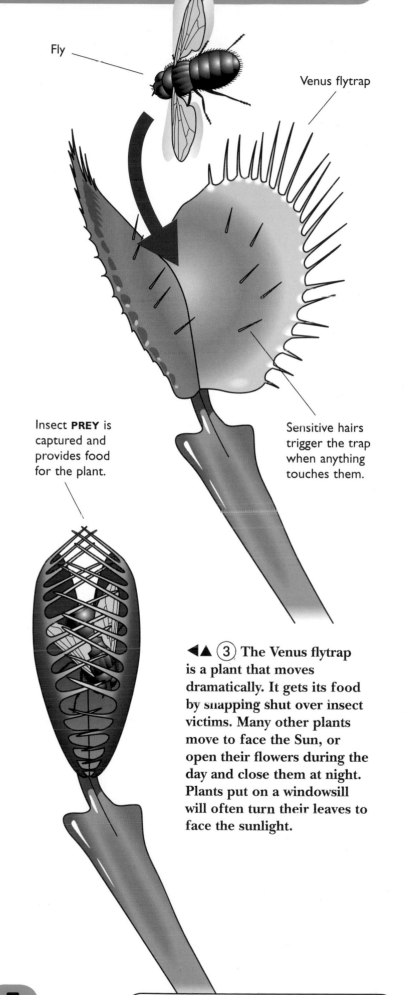

Fly

Venus flytrap

Insect **PREY** is captured and provides food for the plant.

Sensitive hairs trigger the trap when anything touches them.

◄▲ ③ The Venus flytrap is a plant that moves dramatically. It gets its food by snapping shut over insect victims. Many other plants move to face the Sun, or open their flowers during the day and close them at night. Plants put on a windowsill will often turn their leaves to face the sunlight.

end of the scale, living things can be so small that it takes a powerful microscope just to see them, as is the case with tiny creatures called **MICRO-ORGANISMS**, or microbes.

It is not always easy to prove that some things are living. Look, for example, at a lichen (which is actually two different plant-like things growing very close together) growing on a stone (picture ②). The lichen doesn't seem to move, is often dry and crisp to the touch and it grows by less than a millimetre a year, so it looks much the same for a long time. In fact, to many people, it would appear to be a non-living thing, like a stain on the rock.

What living things share

Lichens, humans, trees, whales and all other living things have certain things in common:

▶ They take in food to make **ENERGY** (picture ③).

▶ They give off waste products, even if this is only heat or a gas.

▶ They grow, even if slowly.

▶ They can move, even if only a little.

▶ They are affected by changes in the world around them (called their **ENVIRONMENT**).

▶ They change, or **ADAPT**, over time to suit their environment.

▶ They can make new living things (such as babies) of their own kind.

Changes through their lives

During their lives, all living things go through stages as they grow up, get older and die. At each stage they have to be adapted to the environment around them.

Living things all share the same pattern: they are born, they grow up and they die. This is called a **LIFE CYCLE** (picture ①).

Everything that has ever lived has had a life cycle. In some living things the life cycle can be very long. Some trees live for thousands of years. But many living things have much shorter life cycles. Some insects have a life cycle of just a few days.

Adapting to threats

At each stage of their lives, many living things may take on a different form, or may be threatened in quite different ways. For example, the tree begins as a **SEED**. At this stage it may be eaten, so plants either scatter many seeds, or they protect their seeds so they will pass unharmed through most animals.

▼ ① **This is a life cycle of a plant. It shows the stages of life of a coniferous tree – the kind we often use for Christmas trees. You can think of it starting with the sprouting of new seeds (1).**

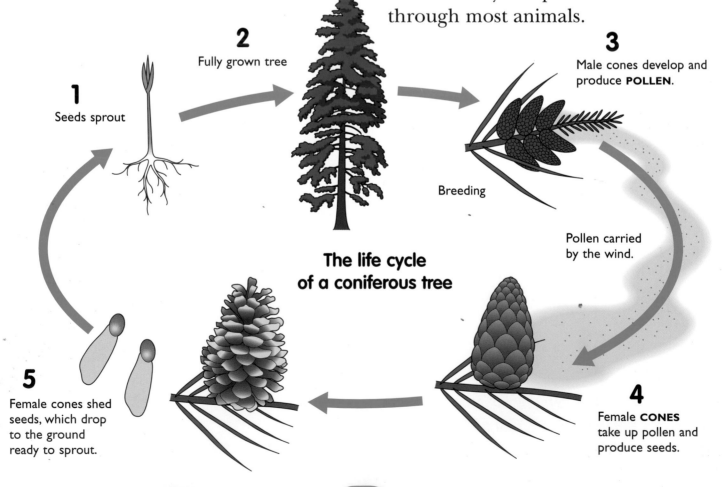

1 Seeds sprout

2 Fully grown tree

3 Male cones develop and produce **POLLEN**.

Breeding

Pollen carried by the wind.

The life cycle of a coniferous tree

4 Female **CONES** take up pollen and produce seeds.

5 Female cones shed seeds, which drop to the ground ready to sprout.

This beautiful morpho butterfly is from Central America. This is an adult. It only lives for 15 days, in which time it has to find a mate.

The female morpho butterfly lays eggs on leaves of the plant that the caterpillar will like to eat when it hatches.

Male and female butterfly breed. Female produces eggs.

A morpho caterpillar **MOULTS** several times as it grows. Each time it changes shape and colour.

The life cycle of a butterfly

Fully grown adult butterfly with wings.

After a few more weeks the adult morpho butterfly emerges from the chrysalis.

LARVA (for butterflies the larva is called a caterpillar).

PUPA (for butterflies the pupa is called a chrysalis).

When it has finished growing, the caterpillar finds a suitable place to pupate. It changes into a pupa.

▲ ② The life cycle of a butterfly, showing the many different forms and adaptations that it takes on during its life.

When they are young saplings, trees may be eaten or trampled on. Similarly, young animals may be eaten by other animals.

Many animals, for example the butterflies shown in picture ②, begin as **EGGS** and have to be hidden from sight. Then they grow into one form (a caterpillar, for example) and finally change to another form (the butterfly). At each stage the plant or animal needs a different way of surviving.

If they survive the first days and weeks, they grow rapidly and are soon more able to defend themselves.

How plants adapt and survive

If a plant is to get through its life cycle, it has to have ways of staying alive and getting its seeds to thrive.

All living things survive over time only if they can stay alive long enough to produce at least one offspring to replace each adult.

This is not as easy as it sounds. Many things can prevent a plant from producing **SEEDS**, or destroy the seeds.

The poppy (picture ①) is an example of a plant that completes its entire life cycle in one year (called an **ANNUAL**). It therefore has just one chance of successfully producing a new generation. How does it do this? By producing as many seeds in a year as a long-lived plant (called a **PERENNIAL**) may produce in a century.

▼ ① **This is the life cycle of the poppy. It is typical of many short-lived flowering plants.**

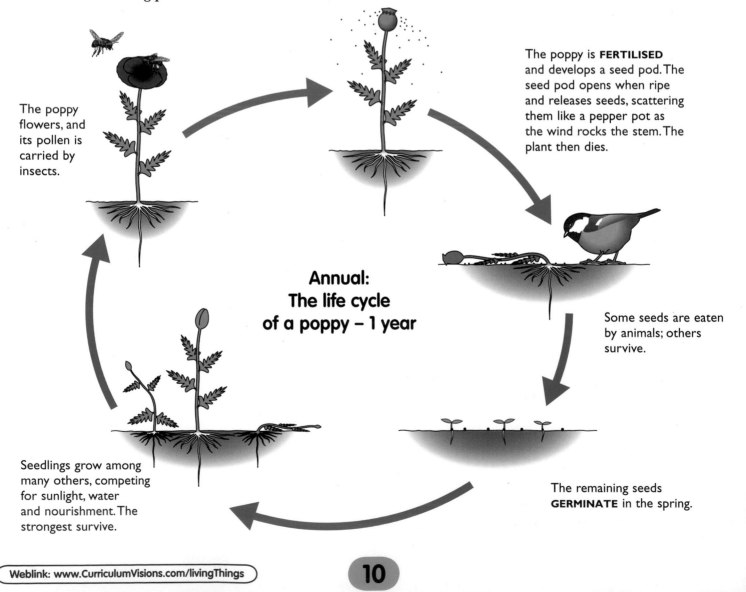

The poppy flowers, and its pollen is carried by insects.

The poppy is **FERTILISED** and develops a seed pod. The seed pod opens when ripe and releases seeds, scattering them like a pepper pot as the wind rocks the stem. The plant then dies.

**Annual:
The life cycle
of a poppy – 1 year**

Some seeds are eaten by animals; others survive.

Seedlings grow among many others, competing for sunlight, water and nourishment. The strongest survive.

The remaining seeds **GERMINATE** in the spring.

▼ ② **Bracken and some of its many defences.**

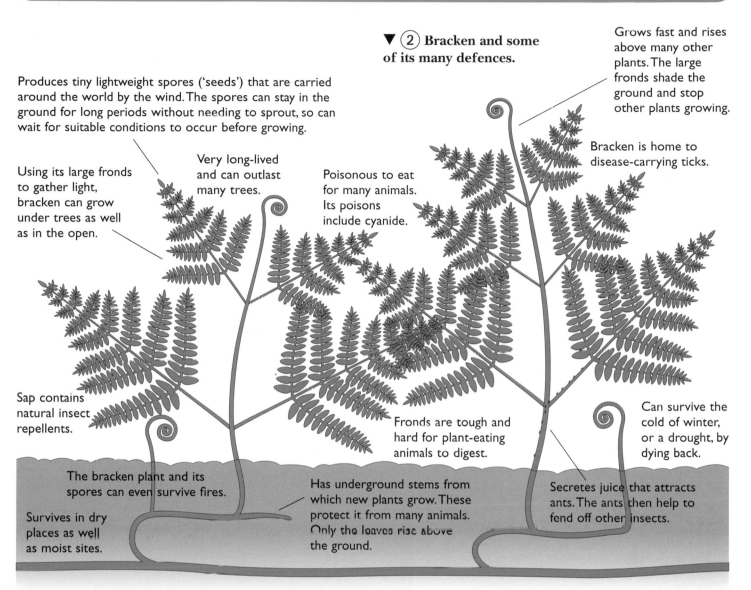

Produces tiny lightweight spores ('seeds') that are carried around the world by the wind. The spores can stay in the ground for long periods without needing to sprout, so can wait for suitable conditions to occur before growing.

Grows fast and rises above many other plants. The large fronds shade the ground and stop other plants growing.

Using its large fronds to gather light, bracken can grow under trees as well as in the open.

Very long-lived and can outlast many trees.

Poisonous to eat for many animals. Its poisons include cyanide.

Bracken is home to disease-carrying ticks.

Sap contains natural insect repellents.

Fronds are tough and hard for plant-eating animals to digest.

Can survive the cold of winter, or a drought, by dying back.

The bracken plant and its spores can even survive fires.

Survives in dry places as well as moist sites.

Has underground stems from which new plants grow. These protect it from many animals. Only the leaves rise above the ground.

Secretes juice that attracts ants. The ants then help to fend off other insects.

How plants protect themselves

As well as having many ways of scattering their seeds, plants have many ways of protecting themselves from attack. Some plants have poisons in their leaves or needles so that hungry animals will avoid them (picture ②). Others surround themselves with sharp spines or thorns (picture ③).

If all this fails, and the leaves still get eaten, or the branches destroyed by wind or fire, then plants will grow new shoots from just below the damaged area.

▼ ③ **A rose plant defends itself with the thorns on its branches. It also grows new shoots very quickly if old branches are damaged.**

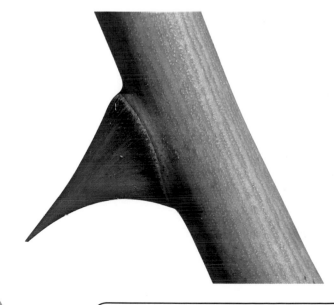

How animals survive

Unlike plants, which cannot move and have to protect themselves where they grow, animals can move about to find food and protect themselves.

Wild animals are very sensible about what they eat. Just like us, they sense that some foods are good for them. They know that their bodies can only digest certain foods. This is why animals search for the foods that suit them best. An animal will starve if it cannot find suitable food, even if there are other types of food around.

▼ ① **This is the skull of a deer. Deer feed entirely on plants and need to be able to cut and grind the tough fibres in their food.**

The incisors and canines are only present in the lower jaw. The upper jaw has a tough pad. The teeth and the pad act like a knife and chopping board when the animal bites grass. The back teeth have many ridges which grind up the food as the jaw moves from side to side.

Plant eaters

Many animals can only get the correct diet by eating plants (picture ①). Some of the world's largest animals, such as the elephant and the giraffe, are plant eaters (**HERBIVORES**).

There are large numbers of plant eaters in every part of the world. These may be insects such as grasshoppers, seed-eating birds such as finches, or small animals such as squirrels, which eat fruits, nuts and the bark from trees (picture ②).

Molars

Incisors and canines

Meat eaters

Some animals can only get the right food by eating other animals (picture ③).

We tend to think of meat eaters (**CARNIVORES**) as large animals such as lions and tigers. But smaller animals, such as frogs and hawks, are meat eaters, too. These animals cannot use plants for food because they cannot digest plants.

◄ ② For squirrels, acorns are an important source of food.

Meat and plant eaters

Only a few animals can get nourishment from both plants and other animals. The bear and the wild boar are two animals that eat both meat and plants.

Surviving

Only the largest meat eaters are safe from being eaten by others. To survive, smaller animals must be able to run or hide. Some, such as squirrels, escape by going up trees. As a result, they are found only in forests. Others, such as deer, can run fast and are **CAMOUFLAGED**. They also protect themselves by living in herds.

Incisors

Canines

Molars

▲ ③ Wolves hunt in packs and eat meat. When they catch their prey they have to tear up the flesh. The wolf's front teeth are large and sharp so that it can hold on to its prey and bring it to the ground. The back teeth are more pointed than human teeth because they are used in tearing. Wolves do not crush their food, but swallow lumps whole.

Weblink: www.CurriculumVisions.com/livingThings

Living together

Many plants and animals share the same living area even though this can also mean danger.

A nice, sunny rock close to a stream may be shared by many living things. For example, some small plants may grow on it, or it may be a resting place for dragonflies. But it is also a good place for lizards and other reptiles to sun themselves and warm up (picture ①).

When you look around, you find many different kinds of living things. Each different kind of living thing is called a **SPECIES**. Species are groups that breed together. Each species that you see in an area is using that place as part of its home.

How many things can live together?

Every living thing has to have a home where it can find food. In the case of plants, this means that there has to be enough nourishment in the soil, sunlight and water for their needs. Some plants need a lot of food and water, while others can live in areas with poor soils.

Animals have to find somewhere with enough plants, or other animals, to eat. Some animals will eat many different types of plants or animals,

▼ ① **These terrapins are fish eaters, so they live by lakes and rivers, but because they are cold-blooded, they also have to find sunny places to warm up.**

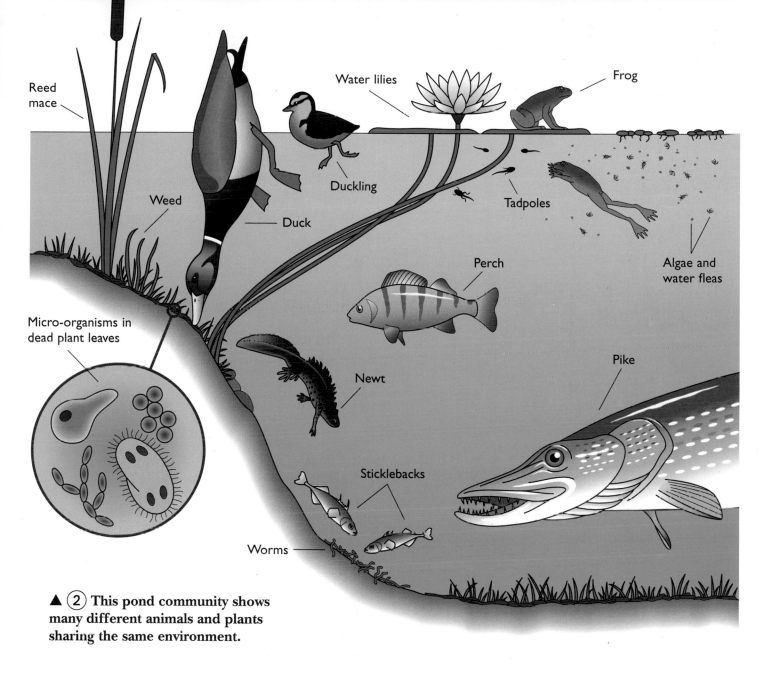

Reed mace

Water lilies

Frog

Weed

Duck

Duckling

Tadpoles

Algae and water fleas

Perch

Micro-organisms in dead plant leaves

Newt

Pike

Sticklebacks

Worms

▲ ② **This pond community shows many different animals and plants sharing the same environment.**

others eat only one type of food. The panda, for example, eats just bamboo, while most bears will eat fruit, insects, fish and other animals.

In general, a place where there is good soil, warm, sunny conditions and enough water will be home to many living things. This means that many plants or animals of the same kind, or of different kinds, will live there.

Communities

All of the living things in an area make up a **COMMUNITY**. The community is entirely self-contained. It does not need anything from outside except water, air and sunlight. So, communities of plants and animals can all share the same home (picture ②).

Food chains

Many of the plants and animals that live together in a community depend on each other as a source of food, or to help them breed.

All life must eat to survive. As a result, each of the species in a community must find enough to eat. They must also breed to continue the species.

Plants and animals

Plants produce more living material than anything else in the community. However, many plants also need animals to help spread their **POLLEN** and to carry their seeds to new areas where they can grow.

▼ ① **Examples of food chains on land. Some animals belong to more than one food chain. This is shown by the cross-over arrows.**

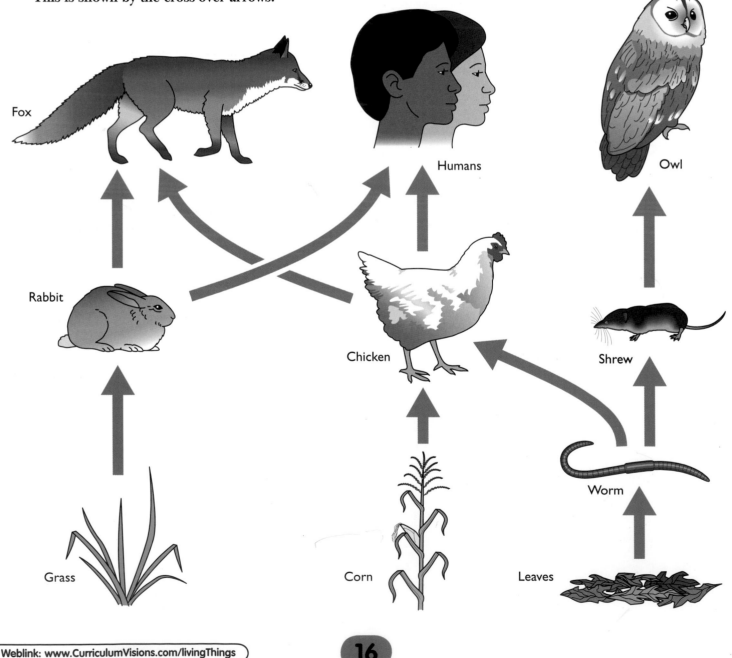

Fox

Humans

Owl

Rabbit

Chicken

Shrew

Grass

Corn

Leaves

Worm

Checks and balances

There must be a way for plants and animals to survive. Nature's way is to make sure that no one kind of living thing is entirely wiped out by another.

You can understand how this works by imagining a forest edge where there are grasses, rabbits and foxes (picture ①). Rabbits are plant eaters, and foxes are meat eaters.

In a good year the grass may grow strongly and so there is plenty of food for the rabbits. So, the rabbits breed well. Now there is more food for the foxes, so they breed well, too. But if there are too many rabbits and they eat all of the grass, the grass will not grow up and many rabbits will starve. With fewer rabbits to eat, the fox numbers will also go down. Now there is a chance for the grass to grow up again.

Food chain

As you can see, in nature there is a long line of animals, each depending on another animal or a plant for its food. Scientists call this a **FOOD CHAIN**.

Picture ② shows a typical food chain for part of a pond:

Pond weed ➤ tadpole ➤ perch ➤ pike

Notice that when the chain is written in words, the plant is on the left and the pike (the last link in the chain) is on the right.

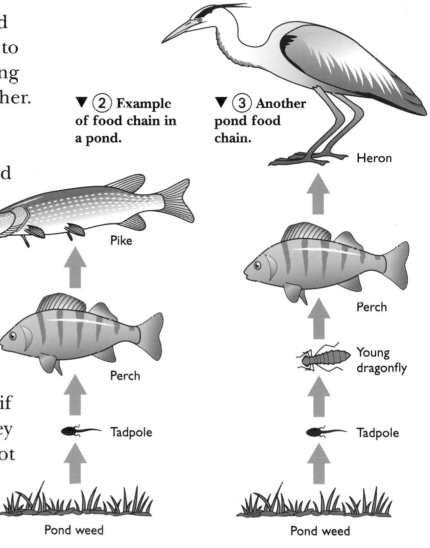

▼ ② Example of food chain in a pond.

▼ ③ Another pond food chain.

Heron

Pike

Perch

Perch

Young dragonfly

Tadpole

Tadpole

Pond weed

Pond weed

Any community will have lots of food chains. Picture ③ shows another pond example:

Pond weed ➤ tadpole ➤ young dragonfly ➤ perch ➤ heron

Harder words

You may want to remember these words:
- Plant-eating animals are called HERBIVORES.
- Meat-eating animals are called CARNIVORES.
- Animals that hunt other animals are called PREDATORS.
- Animals that are hunted are called PREY.
- A food web is the term for a number of interlinked food chains.

A tree as a home

Every living thing has to find a place where it can live, find food and protect itself from others. Here is what happens in an oak tree.

Just like us, animals and plants have a place where they live – a kind of home. We call this natural home a **HABITAT**.

A fully-grown oak tree may be 30 to 35 metres tall and spread its branches nearly as wide (picture ①). Its many leaves allow it to soak up the light that it needs to make its own food, and it gets water and other nourishment from the ground. The oak tree survives where it does because it is adapted to cope with a cold winter (see page 20).

Many lodgers

The oak tree provides a home for more kinds of animal than any other woodland tree (picture ②). Scientists have counted 30 different kinds of birds and over 200 different kinds of moth in just one oak tree!

How does the tree cope with all these hungry lodgers eating its leaves and fruits (acorns)? A single oak tree produces up to a hundred thousand acorns a year. With so many, some are bound not to get eaten. Each oak needs only one of the acorns it has produced to grow into a tree each century for the woodland to survive.

▶ ① The life cycle of an oak. An oak lives for many years and is an example of a PERENNIAL plant. It grows and sets seed year after year even though it is home and food for so many animals.

Oak trees use the wind to share pollen, but use birds and animals to help **DISPERSE** acorns. After hundreds of years the tree finally dies.

The life cycle of an oak

Acorns drop from the tree. Most are eaten, or are destroyed by disease or insects, but a few survive.

Many seedlings are eaten by animals or insects. The ones that survive grow slowly into mature trees.

Acorns grow up into new trees.

Small birds called tits fly among the branches, feeding on caterpillars. Leaves offer protection from birds of prey.

Owls use the tree for roosting and as a place from which to swoop down on other animals.

Pigeons roost on branches and eat acorns.

Woodpeckers search the bark for insects using a strong, hammer-like beak.

Caterpillars feed on leaves. CAMOUFLAGE offers them protection from the birds.

Deer use oak woodland for grazing. The shelter of the trees makes it easier for them to hide from hunters.

Wasps irritate leaves to make them produce hollow 'galls' in which the wasps lay their eggs.

The agile sparrow hawk finds small birds such as tits among the oak branches.

Fungus lives on dead branches.

Squirrel

Bluebells, anemones and other small plants live below the tree.

▲ ② An oak tree provides many places that can be used as homes. Beetles live in the roots, in the cracks of the bark and some even burrow under the bark and into the wood. Caterpillars munch away at the soft leaves.

The angles of the branches make roosting and nesting sites for birds. Natural hollows provide homes for squirrels, owls and even bats.

Woodland through the seasons

A woodland changes dramatically through the seasons. The lives of both plants and animals are adapted to the changes.

You have already seen how a single oak tree can be a home for many animals. When many oaks grow together they make an oak woodland. Here you can see, all in one place, many of the ways of adapting described on the previous pages (picture ①).

The canopy

Oaks grow until their branches fit together to make a covering of leaves called a **CANOPY**. This is how the leaves get the light they need from the Sun.

The canopy is thick with leaves and acorns for part of the year, but in winter the leaves are gone and the branches bare, windswept and cold.

The woodland floor

Many plants and animals live below the canopy. Buds, leaves, flowers, falling fruit and nuts are all food for animals that live on the woodland floor.

Adapting to the seasons

Because the food supply of the woodland changes so much with

▼ ① **An oak woodland through the four seasons.**

Winter

Birds adapted to the cold feed on seeds, berries and shoots in the undergrowth.

Insects survive as eggs. Many stay in the soil or shelter under leaves or bark until spring.

Holly bush produces berries.

Snowdrop

Squirrels use the nuts they stored in autumn.

Hedgehog hibernates in bracken.

Spring

First leaves start to sprout on trees.

Birds attracted to insects on tree.

Birds that are not adapted to the cold winter return from winter homes in warmer parts of the world.

Caterpillars hatch from eggs.

Bluebells begin to flower.

Primrose flowering is almost over.

the seasons, the way the animals behave also changes.

Many insects spend the winter as eggs or **PUPAE** (picture ②) because they have no leaves to eat. Hedgehogs can eat worms, slugs, spiders and insects. But as their food supply dwindles, hedgehogs **HIBERNATE** and sleep during most of the winter season.

Wood mice do not hibernate. They eat seeds and bark in the winter, and buds and seedlings in spring when the plants begin to shoot. They also eat insects during the summer, and blackberries and mushrooms in autumn. Squirrels survive the winter on the acorns and other seeds they buried in the ground during the autumn.

▶ ② This superbly camouflaged butterfly chrysalis (a kind of pupa) is about two centimetres long. It hangs in the shelter of a twig, branch or leaf. In the winter, many adult moths and butterflies die, but their offspring spend the winter as an egg or as a pupa, often underground.

The woodland has far fewer birds in winter because many **MIGRATE** (fly away) to warmer lands. Blue tits and other birds that stay for the winter are adapted to survive the cold and the scarce food supplies.

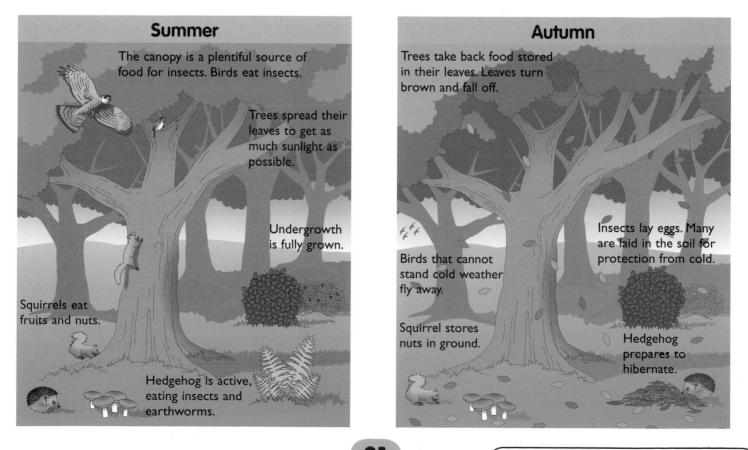

Summer

The canopy is a plentiful source of food for insects. Birds eat insects.

Trees spread their leaves to get as much sunlight as possible.

Undergrowth is fully grown.

Squirrels eat fruits and nuts.

Hedgehog is active, eating insects and earthworms.

Autumn

Trees take back food stored in their leaves. Leaves turn brown and fall off.

Birds that cannot stand cold weather fly away.

Squirrel stores nuts in ground.

Insects lay eggs. Many are laid in the soil for protection from cold.

Hedgehog prepares to hibernate.

Habitats change through the seasons

Many different plants can live in the same place if they grow and flower at different times of the year.

Every kind of living thing needs water, warmth and nourishment. Plants also need light. So how do so many kinds of living things share the same place (habitat)?

In fact, many living things are able to use the same space if they use it in different ways or at different times of the year. In picture ① you can see how different plants use the same woodland through the year.

Growing early

Some plants even begin to grow in winter. Snowdrops are the first to shoot, sometimes even flowering while snow is still on the ground. As the months pass, they are followed by other plants.

The first plants grow from **BULBS**, **TUBERS** and thick underground stems. They use the food they have stored from the previous year. They do not need to wait for the ground to warm up, or the sun to shine strongly, in order to begin their annual growth.

So, by late spring the early plants have all flowered and set seeds almost before the other plants have even started putting out leaves.

▼ ① **Seasonal changes on the forest floor.**

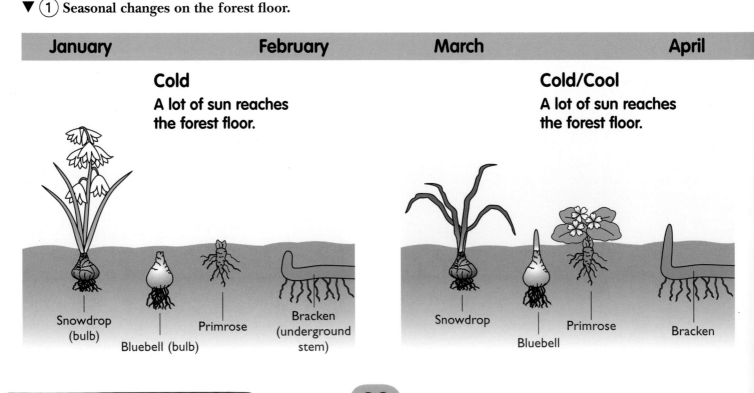

◀ ② This picture, taken in May, shows bluebells already fading by the time the brackens develop their first fronds. Notice that the lower flowers have already turned into green seed pods. Now the leaves will wither as the plant takes the nourishment back into its bulb that it will need for next spring. The first leaves on the trees can also be seen in the background.

Summer leaves

By late spring, the forest floor has warmed up enough for more plants to begin to shoot (picture ②).

Summer woodland plants, such as bracken, do not have bulbs and so do not have a large store of nourishment. This is why it takes them more time to start growing.

But just as these new plants burst into life, trees also start putting out leaves and the ground becomes shady. Summer plants therefore have to be good at growing in the shade. They have adapted to live in a partly shady place. This is why they have leaves that last for many months, so they have longer to make the food that will help their roots below the surface grow.

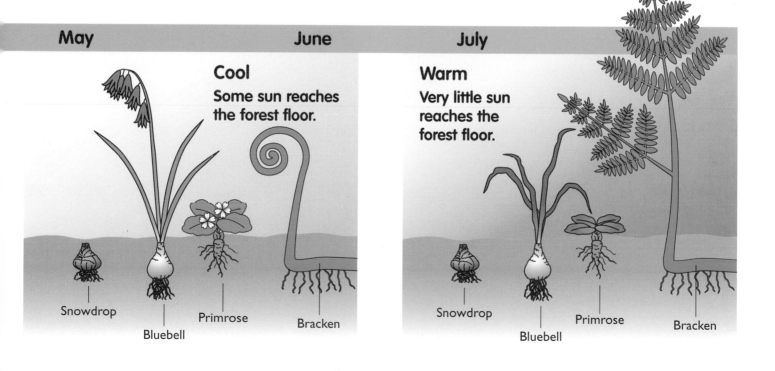

May   **June**

Cool
Some sun reaches the forest floor.

Snowdrop
Bluebell
Primrose
Bracken

July

Warm
Very little sun reaches the forest floor.

Snowdrop
Bluebell
Primrose
Bracken

Weblink: www.CurriculumVisions.com/livingThings

Ponds

Ponds contain still water. The water is shallow at the edge and deeper in the middle, giving lots of opportunities for different kinds of life.

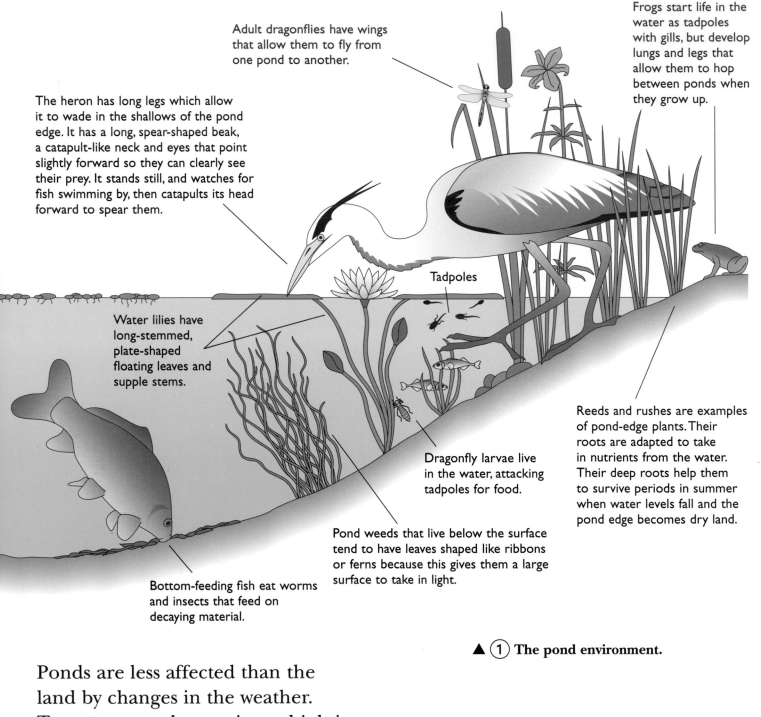

Adult dragonflies have wings that allow them to fly from one pond to another.

Frogs start life in the water as tadpoles with gills, but develop lungs and legs that allow them to hop between ponds when they grow up.

The heron has long legs which allow it to wade in the shallows of the pond edge. It has a long, spear-shaped beak, a catapult-like neck and eyes that point slightly forward so they can clearly see their prey. It stands still, and watches for fish swimming by, then catapults its head forward to spear them.

Water lilies have long-stemmed, plate-shaped floating leaves and supple stems.

Tadpoles

Reeds and rushes are examples of pond-edge plants. Their roots are adapted to take in nutrients from the water. Their deep roots help them to survive periods in summer when water levels fall and the pond edge becomes dry land.

Dragonfly larvae live in the water, attacking tadpoles for food.

Pond weeds that live below the surface tend to have leaves shaped like ribbons or ferns because this gives them a large surface to take in light.

Bottom-feeding fish eat worms and insects that feed on decaying material.

▲ ① The pond environment.

Ponds are less affected than the land by changes in the weather. Temperatures do not rise so high in the day, nor fall so far at night. In winter, only the surface of the pond freezes over.

This means that pond life does not have to adapt so much to the weather in order to survive (picture ①).

Plants in a pond

Ponds do not have many large plants in them. But they still contain food for animals. You may be surprised to know that the pond is full of plants you cannot see. This is because most of the plants are tiny, and usually only visible with a microscope. They are called **ALGAE** (picture ②).

The larger plants are mostly rooted in the pond mud. The plants that live around the edge of the pond have only their roots in water, and their stems and leaves in the air.

Farther from the edge are the plants that have leaves floating on the surface, but stems and roots in the water. The stems do not need to be stiff, because they are supported by the water.

Finally, there are plants that live totally beneath the surface but still have roots in the pond bottom. These are the pond weeds. They still need light, so they must stay close to the surface, but they get everything else they need from the water.

Animals in a pond

Most of the food in a pond is tiny algae. Lots of small animals, such as water fleas, eat the algae.

These plant-eating animals are, in turn, prey to bigger pond animals, such as insects, fish, frogs and birds.

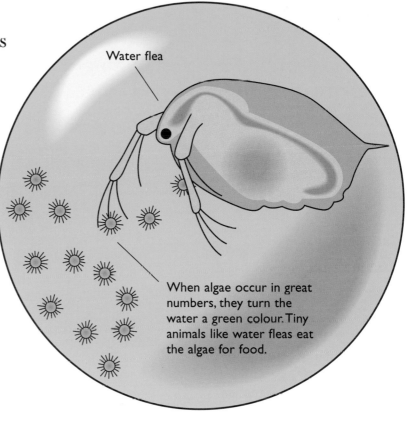

Water flea

When algae occur in great numbers, they turn the water a green colour. Tiny animals like water fleas eat the algae for food.

▲ ② Pond water seen through a microscope.

The smaller animals survive by breeding in huge numbers.

All the waste and dead matter produced by plants and animals settles to the bottom of the pond, where it is used as food for yet more animals. These include many insect **LARVAE**, and some worms and water lice.

All pond animals have to be adapted to moving between ponds to find more space. There are many ways they do this. Frogs, for example, change from water-living tadpoles to air-breathing frogs. By contrast, the eggs of fish stick to the feet of birds that fly between ponds.

Rivers

Rivers often begin as fast-flowing streams with stony beds, then get slower and flow over muddy beds as they near the sea. As a result, rivers contain many different types of life.

Rivers flow from high land, where they have stony beds, to lowlands, where their beds are made of mud and silt, to the sea, where rivers become tidal and where sandbanks and mudflats are common (picture ①). Quite different types of plants and animals are adapted to live in each part of the river's course.

The upper part of a river

Rivers that flow quickly over stony beds sweep many plants and animals away, so most river animals found here are strong swimmers, or can shelter between the rocks (picture ②). Here, animals feed on

Fish such as trout swim strongly but, even so, they prefer the pools, while most smaller creatures have to live in the shelter of rocks.

Dippers can swim in fast-flowing water and eat insect larvae that cling to the stones. They nest in rocky crevices in river banks.

▲ ② The upper reaches of a river, where the bed is stony.

▼ ① The course of a river.

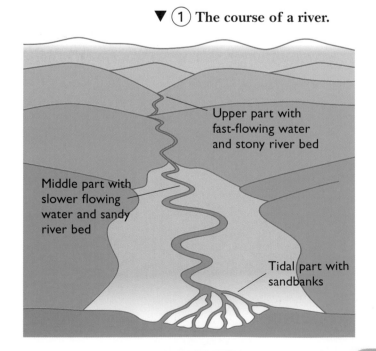

Upper part with fast-flowing water and stony river bed

Middle part with slower flowing water and sandy river bed

Tidal part with sandbanks

leaves falling into the water, or catch insects on or in the water.

The middle part of a river

Downstream, the water flows slowly enough for sand, silt and mud to settle out (picture ③). Many animals have made use of this soft material to protect themselves. Animals such as mussels dig deep burrows. Rooted plants can also grow here.

Most small animals feed on dead leaves that sink to the river bottom.

Otters nest in the bank, using underwater entrances.

Kingfishers nest in holes that they dig for themselves in the outside bank of river channels.

A kingfisher catches food by sitting on a branch overhanging the river and looking for fish and other prey in the water. Then it dives down and catches its food with its strong, pointed stabbing beak before returning to its perch. Kingfishers hunt by day.

Some trout will still be found in this part of the river but bream, chub and barbel are the more common types of fish.

Weeds have their roots in the river mud.

DECOMPOSERS such as snails, worms and insect larvae live on the river bed.

Otters have webbed feet, a waterproof coat and sharp claws and teeth to catch food such as fish. They can even close their ears to stop water getting in.

Kingfisher

▲ ③ The middle reaches of a river, where meanders are cut in soft banks.

More varieties of fish are found here, including those that are less strong swimmers. River banks are soft and provide a home for burrowing birds such as kingfishers, and **MAMMALS** such as otters and water voles.

The tidal part of a river

At the mouth of the river the water is very sluggish and the bottom muds become thick. More plants can take root, and huge numbers of burrowing animals, such as worms and snails, can thrive. Wading birds of all kinds are adapted to find food buried in the sand and mud (picture ④).

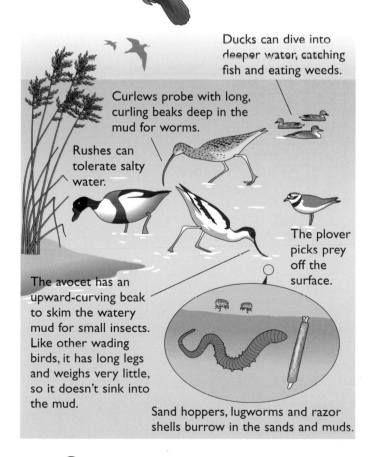

Ducks can dive into deeper water, catching fish and eating weeds.

Curlews probe with long, curling beaks deep in the mud for worms.

Rushes can tolerate salty water.

The plover picks prey off the surface.

The avocet has an upward-curving beak to skim the watery mud for small insects. Like other wading birds, it has long legs and weighs very little, so it doesn't sink into the mud.

Sand hoppers, lugworms and razor shells burrow in the sands and muds.

▲ ④ The tidal reaches of the river, where mudflats and sandbanks are common.

Rock pools

Some animals can live in rock pools, even though they are battered by waves, if they are adapted in the right way.

▼ ① The rock pool environment.

The oystercatcher has a chisel-shaped bill to open limpets, and other shells, or to prise them off rocks.

Limpets have streamlined shells so they are not easily pulled off the rock by breaking waves. Their shells are thick, so they do not crack easily if they are hit by pebbles in the waves.

The sea anemone closes up tight during low tide. It only opens when the sea rises – then it sends out stinging tentacles.

The flexible, waving fronds of seaweeds move with the waves and so are not broken by them. Unlike land plants, they take in all of their nourishment from the sea water through their fronds, instead of their roots.

Starfish can use their feet to hang on to the rocky surface of the pool while waves are breaking.

Tiny algae that float in the sea water are the food for many animals, such as limpets and mussels.

A blenny is a typical, small rock pool fish. It has eyes on top of its head so that it can spot a bird trying to stab it from above. Its mottled colours help to camouflage it among the pebbles at the bottom of the rock pool.

Hermit crabs use empty shells to protect their soft bodies. They eat food that gets washed in by waves.

Rock pools are bowl-shaped hollows which hold sea water when the tide goes out (picture ①).

A rock pool is a very difficult place to live because conditions are continually changing. For example, rock pools can get very hot on a sunny day, and cold at night. When the tide is out, some animals close up so they don't dry out.

Waves and tides

Twice a day – as the tide comes in and as it goes out – plants and animals must be able to stand up to the battering of breaking waves by holding fast to rocks or sheltering in some way (picture ②). Clearly, a rock pool is no place for large living things or those that are in any way delicate.

Animals like crabs, shrimps and small fish take shelter from waves under rocky ledges or stones. Some can burrow into the sandy bottom of the pool.

Finding food

Rock pools do not contain much food, so animals must be able to survive by eating only when the tide comes in. When there is nothing to eat, many animals, such as sea anemones and limpets, close up tight and wait for a new supply of food to arrive with the next tide.

Depending on one another

Each of the creatures in a shallow, seaweed-free rock pool is easy prey for hunters such as birds. This is why larger pools, with lots of seaweed to hide under, are home to more small animals than open pools.

The seaweed has extra benefits. It puts oxygen into the water and so helps more water-life to survive the period between tides. At the same time, the pool animals release wastes that contain the nourishment the seaweed needs. In this way, many of the living things in a rock pool depend on one another.

Offspring

How do living things produce young in such a battering environment? Many send out huge numbers of eggs which hatch in the open sea. Only when the young are almost fully grown do they seek a pool to live in. Others shelter their young until they are grown up enough to fend for themselves.

◄ ② Rock pools at low tide, with waves breaking in the distance. Notice the sandy bed of the pool, and the seaweed. Colonies of mussels are clinging to the bare rock above the pool. Notice how they live together for added protection from the waves.

Mountains

Mountains have cool summers and harsh, snowy winters. They are places where only the specially adapted can survive.

High mountains experience long, cold, snowy winters and short, wet, cloudy summers. Not only is the weather harsh, but soils are thin and stony and have little nourishment in them.

Mountain plants

Few plants can survive such conditions. Some of those that are adapted to cope with the cold and wind are called **ALPINES**. Most alpines are perennials. Few annual plants grow on mountains – it takes many years of slow, determined growth

for a plant just to get big enough to flower (picture ①). Alpines are small, woody perennial plants that hug the ground, or shelter between boulders, growing just a little each year in the brief summer.

Mountain animals

Because mountain plants are scarce and grow slowly, there is not much food for animals on a mountain. Each animal needs a large **TERRITORY** in which to search

▼ ① **How alpine plants are adapted to the harsh mountain environment.**

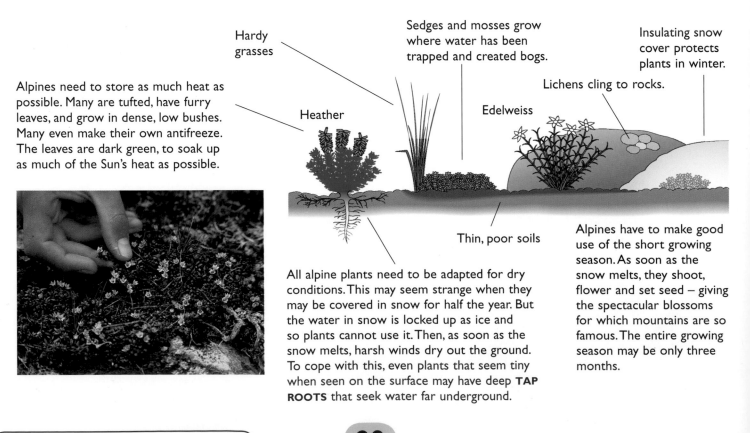

Alpines need to store as much heat as possible. Many are tufted, have furry leaves, and grow in dense, low bushes. Many even make their own antifreeze. The leaves are dark green, to soak up as much of the Sun's heat as possible.

Hardy grasses

Sedges and mosses grow where water has been trapped and created bogs.

Insulating snow cover protects plants in winter.

Lichens cling to rocks.

Heather

Edelweiss

Thin, poor soils

All alpine plants need to be adapted for dry conditions. This may seem strange when they may be covered in snow for half the year. But the water in snow is locked up as ice and so plants cannot use it. Then, as soon as the snow melts, harsh winds dry out the ground. To cope with this, even plants that seem tiny when seen on the surface may have deep **TAP ROOTS** that seek water far underground.

Alpines have to make good use of the short growing season. As soon as the snow melts, they shoot, flower and set seed – giving the spectacular blossoms for which mountains are so famous. The entire growing season may be only three months.

Golden eagle

Few, if any, plants can grow on the bare rocky cliffs on mountain tops.

Great height allows birds of prey to survey a large area – important when prey is scarce.

Cliff caves provide safe nesting sites and 'launch pads' for mountain birds of prey such as eagles and ravens.

Mountain goats are skilled climbers and can climb on near-vertical cliffs to reach patches of vegetation. However, even they must migrate to lower altitudes in winter because the high mountain areas are deeply covered in snow.

In winter, ptarmigan do not hibernate. They scratch down through the snow to feed on shrubs and lichens. They burrow under the snow to protect themselves from the weather whilst they sleep.

Red deer graze on natural meadows in summer.

Lynx

Raven

Tree line. The upper limit where a forest can grow.

Ptarmigan

Alpine plants

Marmot

Few butterfly species are adapted to high altitudes because they need warmer conditions.

It is common for animals that use camouflage to change their colour with the seasons. Ptarmigan and mountain hare both turn white in winter. In summer, their coats are brown.

The dipper is adapted to fast flowing mountain streams

Apollo butterfly

Mountain hare

▲ ② Some of the many adaptations that animals have to help them survive in the mountains.

Many **RODENTS** in high mountains live in a network of tunnels in the rocky soil. These provide a place to hibernate in winter. However, as rodents such as marmots (above) and voles (below) search among the rocks for food, they are easily spotted by predators such as eagles, weasels, lynx and foxes. To escape being caught, they are camouflaged by the colour of their fur and quickly take shelter in the rocks.

for food (picture ②). A single golden eagle, for example, needs a territory of 200 square kilometres!

Few animals remain in the mountains during winter. Many hibernate until the snow melts in spring. The small number of animals that continue to be active in the winter snow are especially hardy and may change colour to white in order to stay camouflaged in the snow.

Deserts

Deserts are mainly hot places with very little rainfall. Very few plants and animals can survive such difficult conditions.

Deserts are places where the rainfall is small and very unreliable. Most deserts are hot and sunny, so coping with **DROUGHT** is the main problem for any living thing in a desert (picture ①).

Plants with a short life

Plants are adapted in two ways. One group are annuals, whose seeds lie in the desert soil until rain comes. Then, they race to **GERMINATE**, grow, flower and set seed before the ground dries out. This may all happen in just a few weeks.

Plants that grow slowly

The other group of plants are perennials. Between rainfalls they simply stop growing.

Some desert perennials have deep **TAP ROOTS** to find water, even when it has seeped deep underground. To prevent losing water, they have small, waxy leaves with few pores.

Others, such as the cactus, store water in fleshy stems that can swell with water. They have no leaves at all, their green stems make all the food they need.

Animals in the desert

Animals, too, face the problems of getting water, avoiding the heat and finding food. Like mountains, deserts provide little food and so few animals can live there. Those that do each need a large territory if they are to find enough to eat.

Many desert animals burrow into the sand, or shelter in the shade, during the heat of the day, and only come out after dark. At night, the temperature falls sharply and dew is quite common. Many animals get all the moisture they need from the late-night dew.

Camels are one of the few desert animals that move about during the day. Camels can survive when they have lost almost a third of their body water. This is more than twice as much as most animals can lose. When they do find water, camels can drink a fifth of their body weight in ten minutes.

The hump of the camel is where it stores fat. This fat allows it to survive, even if it cannot find food for weeks. Camels also have thick fur to protect them from the heat, and pad-like hooves to make it possible to travel across soft sand.

EXTREME HABITATS

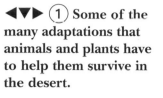

◀▼▶ ① Some of the many adaptations that animals and plants have to help them survive in the desert.

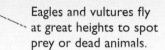

Pincers to grab prey.

Scorpions use the poisonous tip of their tail to kill their prey and defend themselves. They get all of the water they need from the food they eat.

Eagles and vultures fly at great heights to spot prey or dead animals.

The cactus stores water in its stem, has no leaves and has protective spines to stop animals from eating it.

Desert foxes are **NOCTURNAL** scavengers and crafty hunters. They are able to dig out the burrows of kangaroo rats and even eat scorpions. They have large ears and eyes because they only feed at night. They have a keen sense of smell to find rotting meat.

Lizards use camouflage and quick movements to escape hunters.

Sidewinder snakes move across sand in a special way, so that only a small part of their skin rests on the burning hot surface at any time. This way of moving also prevents the snakes from sinking into the soft sand.

Kangaroo rats come out in the cool darkness of the night. Their long legs allow them to run very fast to escape predators such as snakes and foxes. They are adapted to get all the water they need from the moisture in the seeds they eat.

Plants such as the creosote bush have very long tap roots to find water. As with many plants in the desert, they also have small, leathery leaves.

33

Meadows and fields

Many habitats have been changed by people. One of the most common is the meadow. It exists because of the long-term care, or STEWARDSHIP, of the farmer.

▲ ① **This meadow consists of a variety of grasses whose flowers are on the top of tall thin stems. Many other plants can also be seen, including the yellow flower of a buttercup.**

Meadows are places where grasses and other flowering plants thrive, but where trees are rare (picture ①). Natural meadows are only common on high mountains where trees cannot grow. But they are also found in valley bottoms where farmers have cut down the trees to make grazing land for animals (picture ②).

Many varieties of plants

As animals graze, they eat the shoots of trees so new trees can't grow.

Meadows have more variety of grasses and flowering plants than any other place. This is because trees do not shade them out. Over 500 kinds of plants have been found in one meadow.

A wealth of animals

Even though farmers want the meadow to be used for their animals, there is also much wildlife. This is because meadows are a much better place to find food than woodlands.

Many birds nest in among the plants. The skylark is a common meadow bird that eats seeds and insects. It makes its nest on the ground and camouflages it.

Many hunters

With many animals using the meadow for food, meadows attract many winged hunters such as hawks, that patrol by day, or owls, that patrol by night.

Burrowing is one way to make a home that is safe from these hunters. Rabbits and voles are among many burrowing animals that can thrive in a meadow.

Below the surface

The plants on the surface shed lots of leaves that rot and become food for soil animals. The dung of grazing animals can be another source of food. Below the soil there may be tons of earthworms in each hectare of meadow. And there will be a small army of moles and other tunnelling animals trying to eat them. Tunnelling animals like moles have bodies shaped so they can push themselves through the soil. They have strong, short, front legs and spade-like paws with sharp claws so they can dig rapidly.

Kestrels hover and use their keen eyesight to spot their prey, such as mice or voles, among the meadow plants.

▼ ② Animals and plants in a meadow.

Farmers cut meadows and allow animals to graze. This stops trees from growing.

Many perennial plants that grow in meadows sprout from the base of the stem so they can grow back quickly if eaten by grazing animals or cut by farmers.

Perennial grasses and flowering plants thrive because they are not shaded by trees. There are few annual plants in a meadow.

Earthworms are common in soil and eat dead leaves.

Moles have powerful, short legs with claws for digging. Moles can burrow through meadow soil without being troubled by tree roots. There is a plentiful supply of worms for them to eat.

Rabbits and voles dig tunnels in the meadow as protection from owls, kestrels and other hunting birds.

Thoughtless changes

When rivers are cleared out, the habitats for many living things may be lost. This is an example of poor stewardship.

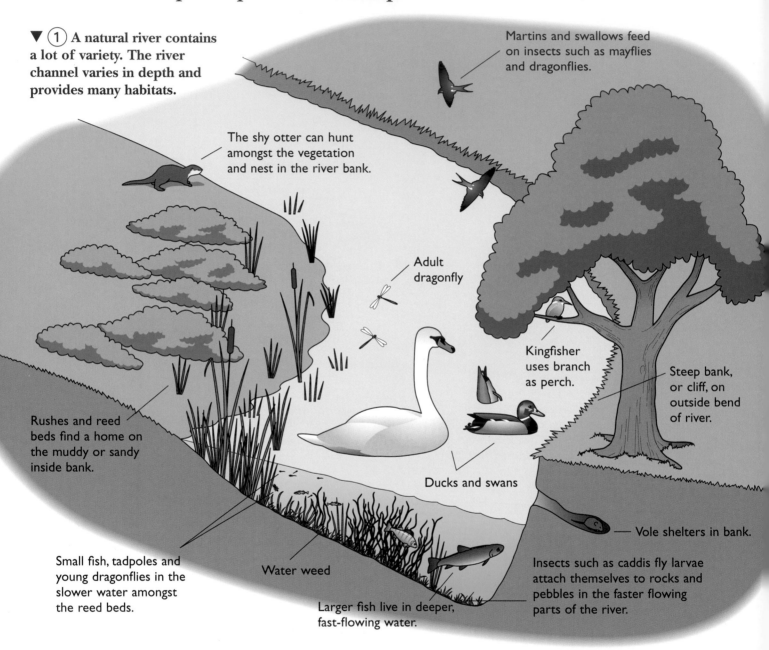

▼ ① A natural river contains a lot of variety. The river channel varies in depth and provides many habitats.

Martins and swallows feed on insects such as mayflies and dragonflies.

The shy otter can hunt amongst the vegetation and nest in the river bank.

Adult dragonfly

Kingfisher uses branch as perch.

Steep bank, or cliff, on outside bend of river.

Rushes and reed beds find a home on the muddy or sandy inside bank.

Ducks and swans

Vole shelters in bank.

Small fish, tadpoles and young dragonflies in the slower water amongst the reed beds.

Water weed

Larger fish live in deeper, fast-flowing water.

Insects such as caddis fly larvae attach themselves to rocks and pebbles in the faster flowing parts of the river.

Rivers are a common part of our landscape. But they can be changed dramatically. This happens when people get worried about rivers flooding, want to use rivers for boats, or want to use the fertile land near the river for farming, but forget that the river environment is home to other living things.

Natural rivers and river banks

Picture ① shows a part of a meandering river that has been undisturbed by humans. The banks

▼ ② A river that has been straightened and cleaned out.

Meadows

Ducks can feed on the green microbes called algae that grow in the water, but they have no protected place to nest.

Tadpoles and fish can be found, but only in small numbers. The variety of fish will be small.

There are few dead leaves on the bottom for insects and other creatures to eat. As a result, there is not much food for fish. There is only a small supply of fish for birds such as kingfishers.

There is little variety of plants on or in the river. There is no place for a kingfisher to perch while hunting for fish.

are undisturbed and lined with trees. You can find a large variety of animals here, and you should be able to make out some food chains. The main features are the fast and slow-flowing areas, deep and shallow areas and open and shaded areas. It is this variety that gives many different species a chance to thrive.

Changing channels

Engineers sometimes straighten and dredge rivers because they believe it will make flooding less likely. They scrape the banks clear and smooth out the bed. This makes a channel that carries water away more quickly (it makes a large open drain). But the shelter and variety of places for wildlife are reduced and this means that fewer plants and animals can live in such a place. You will find that many of the food chains in picture ① have links missing in picture ②. Once one link is missing, the whole chain may collapse and other creatures die.

37

Improving the environment

By making country parks we can turn waste ground into places where many species can thrive. It is one example of many ways in which we can be more considerate for other living things while enjoying the world ourselves.

If we want to improve the world for ourselves, we do not have to destroy the world for other living things. Stewardship is possible in almost every case, from a motorway to a gravel pit.

In towns and countryside there are many areas of wasteland. They may be old factory sites, coal mines or gravel pits, for example. Once they are abandoned, a few species survive, but by making careful changes, these areas can teem with wildlife. All that is needed is to understand what homes (habitats) wildlife needs.

▶ ① **The plan of a simple country park based on an abandoned area of coal mining or disused gravel pits.**

Farmland

Wilderness lake

Area where access is deliberately poor

Fishing lake

Boating lake

Car park

Area where access is easy

Designing a country park

Most of us have a country park nearby. Nearly all of them are on reclaimed land (picture ①). Suppose you had to think about turning an area of wasteland into a place that both people and wildlife can enjoy, what would you do?

From the previous pages in this book, you can see that some living things need open ground, some need woodland and others need ponds or rivers. Some need dry soil while others need moist soil. There has to be enough variety to attract different animals and make food chains. Most wildlife also needs to have some protection from people.

Plan for variety

You can make all of these possible, even in a small area. The key idea is to make the place as varied as possible (picture ②). If a part was dug out to make a pond or a lake, any spare soil could make some small hills. With this simple step you have created lots of different types of land for different species to thrive.

If the hills are now planted with trees, then you have the start of a woodland. Leaving strips of land without trees creates open ground for those species that need it.

Adding a path that goes into part of the woodland, across some open ground (picture ③) and beside part of the pond or lake completes the simple plan. This makes it easier for people to visit, and also makes it more likely that they will not go on the rest of the land. In this way, much of the land is left almost undisturbed for the shy creatures to live in

With these simple steps, both people and wildlife can thrive.

◀ ③ A footpath leads from a woodland area across open grassland.

◀ ② An artificial island has been left in this old gravel pit to make a safe home for some waterbirds.

Finding out where plants live

A habitat is the place where a living thing is best suited to live, and where it finds shelter, food and others of its own kind.

Now that we have seen a wide variety of habitats, we can start to investigate them for ourselves.

Habitats come in all shapes and sizes. There are microbes living in our bodies, on our eyes, ears and so on. Most do you no harm, but to them an ear, a mouth or an eye is home – it is their habitat.

On a larger scale, a woodland is home to the trees that live there, but also to all of the other plants and the many animals that use it for food and shelter (picture ①).

Rock pools by the sea, ponds, rivers or coral reefs are all watery habitats.

Where dandelions live

To get used to finding out where something lives, you can begin by walking around, close to your home or school, and looking at the plants you find there. Then notice where they are common and where they are uncommon.

◄▼► ① As you move from a woodland to a meadow and then to a pond, you will find different things making their home in each place. Each place is a different habitat.

Oak tree

Ivy climbing up tree in shade

Ferns in shade

Brambles partially shaded and partly in sunny areas

SHADE

FULL SUN

Look for the bright-yellow dandelion, for example. You should find it on the school playing field, in your garden or in a park.

What do all of these places have in common that a dandelion would like? They are open places with lots of sunshine. Dandelions cannot grow in the shade, so they choose a sunny place for their habitat (picture ②).

Where water lilies live

Water lilies have large leaves that float on water. Many garden ponds have them. You can also see them in the ponds at parks (picture ③).

If you look at a water lily, you will find it has long, floppy stalks. These are good for allowing the leaves to bob up and down in the water, but they do not have the strength to hold the plant up on dry land.

The water lily has roots, so the whole plant doesn't float. The water lily has its habitat in shallow ponds and swamps, not in deep open water.

◀ ② The open ground in this grassy meadow contains dandelions (grey seed heads) and buttercups (yellow flowers) in among the green grass.

▲ ③ The leaves and flowers of a water lily float on the still surface water of a pond.

Open areas have grass, buttercups, daisies and dandelions.

Water lilies in pond

WATER

Investigating mini-habitats

The leaves of a tree or bush can be home to a wide variety of animals.

A branch may seem to be a very exposed place to live, but in fact it is quite sheltered, and the leaves make a tasty meal for many small animals (picture ①). You can see how full of life it is by gently shaking a branch over a tray (picture ②). Many

▲ ② If you gently shake a branch over a tray, all sorts of small animals will fall out. Try to find out what each of them is. See how many different kinds of animal are using the branch as a home.

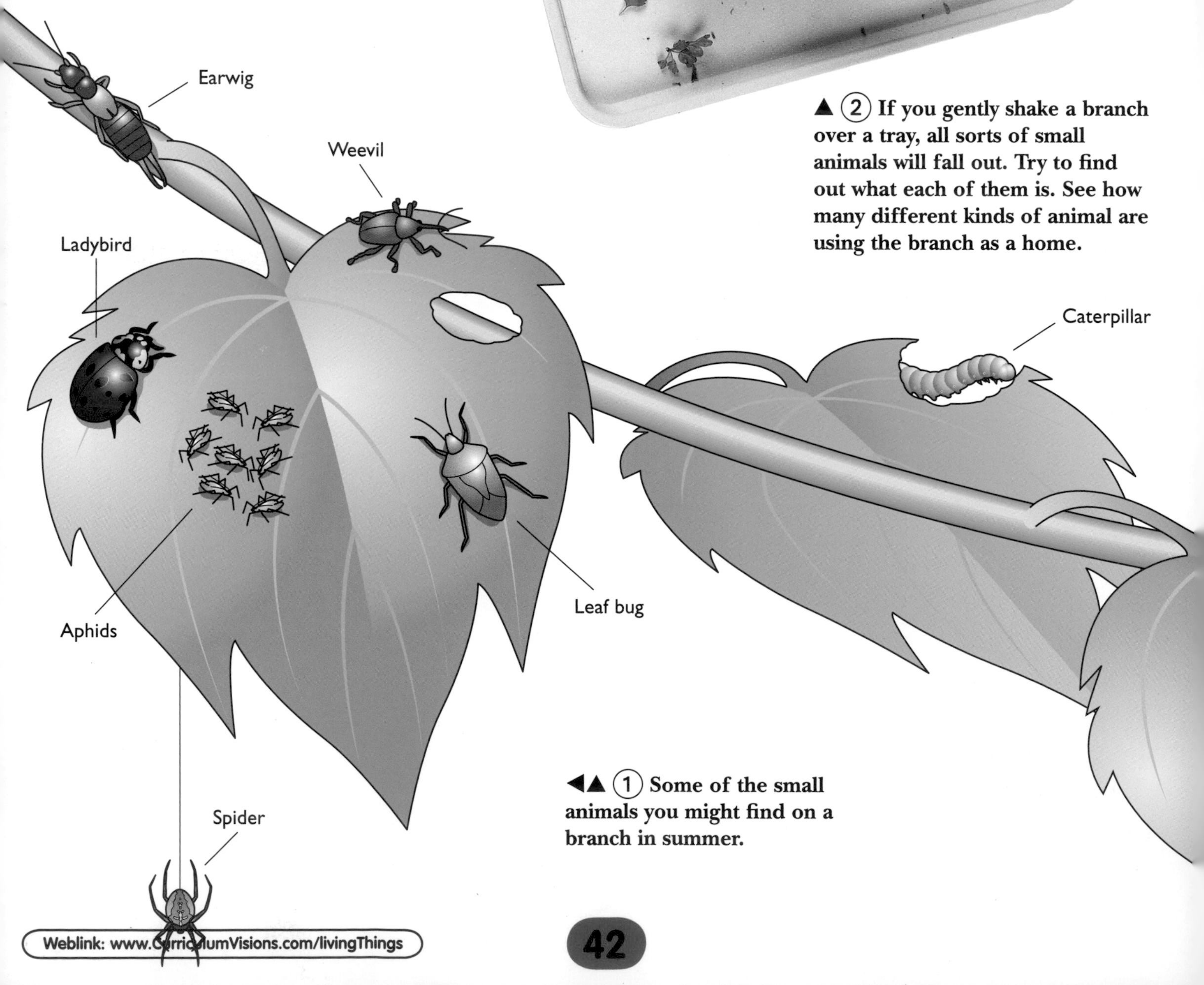

Earwig

Weevil

Ladybird

Caterpillar

Aphids

Leaf bug

Spider

◄▲ ① Some of the small animals you might find on a branch in summer.

animals will fall out, but the chances are you didn't notice any of them before they were shaken free. This is because many of the animals are a colour similar to the leaves they use as a home.

Plant eaters

Some of the animals that live on branches eat leaves. Caterpillars are one example (picture ③). Greenfly (aphids) suck the sap from the leaves. Earwigs are also common on branches. They eat leaves as well.

Many little beetles, such as weevils, can be found on branches too. Weevils are plant eaters.

If you notice a small, black, ball-shaped thing stuck onto a leaf, then you have found a gall. This is where a small wasp lays an egg. It also causes the leaf to produce a swelling around the egg. This is the gall. The larva develops inside, protected by the hard gall.

Hunters

The leaves are also home to animals that hunt. You may, for example, notice a ladybird. It is a hunter, out to eat the aphids.

▲ ③ **If you find a caterpillar on a branch, you can keep it for a short while in a ventilated box with some of the leaves you found it on, and some leaves from different trees. You can then look to see which leaves the caterpillar prefers to eat. In this way you can find out if it depends on a particular tree.**

Lots of tiny spiders can be spotted as well. All spiders are hunters, trying to catch the plant eaters while they graze.

Of course, not everything that uses a branch as its home will fall when you shake it. Many birds live among the leaves. And now that you have seen how many animals there are in among the branches, you can see how birds can easily find enough to eat.

Investigating the variety

If you gently shake branches from a number of bushes and trees growing in the same area over a tray, you will probably find different animals each time. This shows that many animals choose particular plants for their home.

In the soil

A huge variety of life and many habitats can be found in the upper layers of the soil.

When you walk across open ground, you may think that there is nothing below your feet. But hidden out of sight in every soil there are huge numbers of animals that make the soil their home (picture ①).

Underground homes

Why would an animal want to live underground? Plants all have their roots in the soil. The surface of the ground is also where all dead leaves and seeds fall, and where dead animals lie. This provides a plentiful supply of food for many creatures. The soil also gives shelter from the cold and heat.

But, of course, it is much more difficult to move around inside the

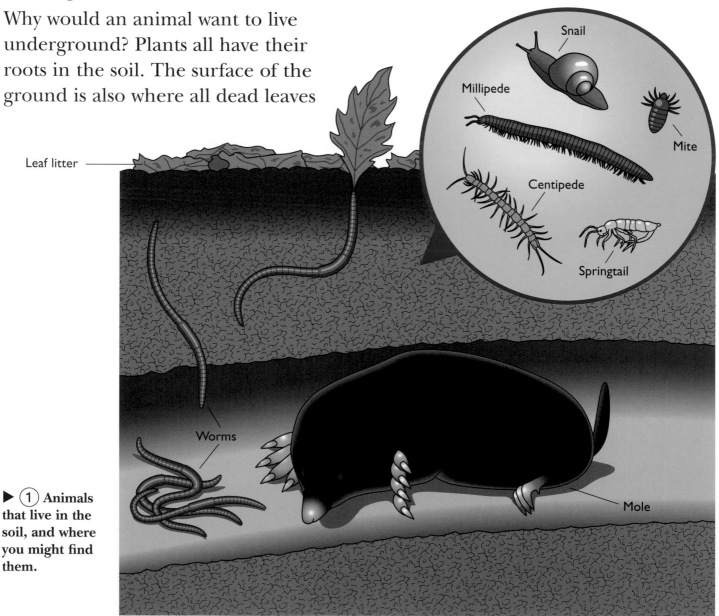

Leaf litter

Snail

Millipede

Mite

Centipede

Springtail

Worms

Mole

▶ ① Animals that live in the soil, and where you might find them.

soil than in the air or in water. So animals must have special shapes that allow them to burrow about. If they are small, animals can also move around among the dead leaves and still keep largely out of sight.

Where earthworms live

Earthworms eat dead plants and animals. They also burrow their way through the soil by eating it. An earthworm eats about its own weight of soil and food each day.

There is no point in an earthworm burrowing too deeply, however, because the deeper parts of soil contain less to eat. So the home (habitat) of an earthworm is in the soil just below the surface – the region we normally call the topsoil.

Where springtails live

Springtails are tiny, wingless insects less than 10mm long. Many are able to spring from place to place, but mostly they crawl about in the leaves that rest on the soil. Springtails eat dead leaves and so they live where the leaves are moist and soft. They do not eat the dried leaves on the surface.

Where moles burrow

Moles are the most common large animals to live entirely in the soil. They eat earthworms and make their home in the topsoil where the earthworms are found.

Dead leaves

Sand

Garden soil

▲ ② A jar is a suitable place to keep worms for a few days. Place a layer of soil at the bottom, then a layer of sand, and a layer of leaves above this. Add two or three worms. You can see how the worms work as they mix the yellow sand with the brown soil.

Investigating the earthworm's home

You can dig out a section of moist soil using a trowel and put it in a glass jar. Place a layer of sand in the jar, then a layer of moist, dead leaves. Place some earthworms on the surface. If you cover the sides of the jar with black paper and keep the soil moist, the earthworms will behave quite normally. If you remove the black paper from time to time, you can see exactly where the earthworms prefer to live (picture ②).

Glossary

ADAPTATION/ADAPT The way in which an animal or plant is suited to where it lives. If something is well adapted to where it lives, it will be more likely to survive.

ALGA (ALGAE) Tiny, plant-like living things, usually freely floating. Algae have a green colouring and get energy from sunlight.

ALPINE The name given to a group of plants that can survive the harsh conditions of high mountains, where there is prolonged snowfall, frequent frost, stony soil, high wind and intense Sun.

ANNUAL Plants that complete their life cycle in one year.

BULB The resting stage of some flowering plants. It consists of a short stem which is surrounded by leaves. The stem is swollen with stored food from the last season's growth. When the correct conditions (such as the warmth of spring) stimulate the plant to start using the stored food, it grows rapidly, pushing out leaves and stalks from the top of the bulb. Lilies, hyacinths and onions are examples of plants with bulbs.

CAMOUFLAGE The pattern of colours and the shape of some animals that allow them to blend in with their surroundings. For example, some moths are coloured and shaped like dead leaves or bark.

CANOPY The high branches of a forest that form a thick layer of leaves. Many insects live in the canopy and never come down to the ground.

CARNIVORE An animal that eats meat.

COMMUNITY The range of living things that occur in the same habitat. For example, different communities of plants and animals will exist in a meadow, an oak wood or a pond.

CONE The equivalent of a flower for conifers. It is a cone-shaped mass of papery scales. Coniferous trees have male cones, which carry pollen, and female cones, which develop seeds.

DECOMPOSER Animals that eat dead material such as dead leaves or dead animals. Scavenging animals, such as magpies, will eat rotting meat. Rotting meat is called carrion. This is a vital role in making sure that the environment stays clean and that the nourishment in dead material is recycled.

DROUGHT An unusually long period without significant rainfall.

EGG A tiny cell that develops in a female animal and that contains half of the instructions needed to make a new life, together with nourishment. Also an immature animal in a shell.

ENERGY The 'power-pack' that makes it possible for living things to grow, move, and so on.

ENVIRONMENT The surroundings in which a living thing finds itself. This will include the type of soil, the shape of the land, the amount of warmth and rain, the amount of shelter and the other plants and animals that share the same space.

FERTILISATION/FERTILISE The joining of male and female sex cells to create a complete set of instructions for a new life.

FOOD CHAIN A group of plants and animals that depend on each other for food. In general, plants need animals to help spread their pollen and seeds. Some animals need plants for food, while other animals need the plant eaters for their food.

GERMINATION/GERMINATE The process in which a seed takes in water and its seed case breaks open to release the root.

HABITAT The place where an animal or plant normally lives. A habitat can be very small (for example, under a leaf) or it may be very large (for example, a tropical rainforest).

HERBIVORE An animal that eats plants for its food.

HIBERNATE To go into a state of very little activity. Hibernating animals sleep for much of the time they are hibernating, but some also wake up and feed from time to time. Hibernation is an adaptation to allow animals to get through a part of the year when there is little food.

LARVA (LARVAE) An early stage of the life cycle of an insect. A caterpillar is an example of a larva.

LIFE CYCLE The series of stages in the growth of a living thing, from fertilisation until death.

MAMMAL A warm-blooded animal that provides milk for its young.

MICRO-ORGANISM An organism that can only be seen with a microscope. Micro-organisms are also called microbes.

MIGRATE To move a long distance in search of food, warmth or a place to breed. Many birds migrate thousands of kilometres, flying between their summer and winter homes.

MOULT In insects, the skin that is shed from time to time in order for them to grow.

NOCTURNAL An animal that is most active at night.

ORGANISM The most general word for any living thing, including both plants and animals.

PERENNIAL A plant that grows a bit more each year and has a lifespan of several years. Trees are the longest-living perennial plants, sometimes living for thousands of years.

PREDATOR An animal that hunts other animals for its food.

POLLEN Yellow grains that are produced by the male parts of a flower.

PREY An animal that is hunted by other animals for food.

PUPA (PUPAE) The stage of the life cycle of an insect between the larva and the adult insect.

RODENT A gnawing animal that has very large, chisel-shaped front teeth. Their teeth are always growing and so are never worn completely away. Rats, mice and squirrels are all rodents.

SEED A miniature plant, together with a supply of food, protected by a hard coating. Seeds of flowering plants form at the base of a flower. As the seed matures, the base of the flower forms a swollen, rounded shape called a fruit.

SPECIES A particular type of living thing. All members of a species look and behave similarly.

STEWARDSHIP The idea that we have a responsibility to keep the natural environment around us from being destroyed or damaged and so allow the planet to continue to support future generations of people and wildlife.

TAP ROOT A thick, central root that anchors the plant and helps the plant collect water.

TERRITORY The region that an animal uses to find its food and to mate. Animals defend their territory in different ways.

TUBER A swelling on a shoot or root in which food is stored.

Index